I Grew Up Poor and Now I Sabotage My Success

I Grew Up Poor and Now I Sabotage My Success

Matthew Petchinsky

1

I Grew Up Poor and Now I Sabotage My Success

By: Matthew Petchinsky

Disclaimer

This book offers psycho-spiritual strategies and reflective practices designed to help readers understand and begin transforming their own patterns of money sabotage, self-limiting beliefs, and inherited scarcity mindsets. The concepts, exercises, and stories presented here are educational and inspirational in nature; they are not a substitute for individualized psychological counseling, psychotherapy, financial planning, or any other form of licensed professional service.

While the methods described may provide insight and relief, every reader's circumstances are unique. If you are experiencing significant financial distress, mental-health challenges, or any situation requiring professional attention, please consult a qualified mental-health practitioner, licensed therapist, certified financial planner, or other relevant specialist. The author and publisher assume no responsibility for decisions made or actions taken by readers based on the material in this book.

All frameworks, rituals, and reflective tools contained herein draw on universal psycho-spiritual principles and secular metaphysical approaches. They intentionally avoid the philosophies, doctrines, and practices of Christianity, Islam, Judaism, or other organized religions. Readers are encouraged to adapt these methods to their own values and beliefs as they see fit.

By reading this book, you acknowledge that you are solely responsible for your own well-being, choices, and financial outcomes, and that the material herein is intended as guidance and inspiration only—not as therapy, legal advice, or financial direction.

Introduction

Escaping poverty is often celebrated as the ultimate victory—but the truth is far more complex. Many who claw their way out of scarcity find themselves haunted by shadows that success alone cannot banish. Money is not just currency; it is memory, emotion, and identity. When you have grown up with hunger in your belly, fear in your home, or shame in your pockets, the story of poverty does not end the moment your bank account grows. It lives on, whispered through the body and etched into the nervous system.

For some, prosperity awakens a strange unease. Achievements feel undeserved. Opportunities spark fear instead of joy. Instead of stepping forward into expansion, an inner hand yanks the emergency brake: *What if I lose it all? What if I betray where I came from? What if I no longer belong?* These questions are not signs of weakness. They are the echoes of survival patterns—deeply ingrained strategies your younger self created to endure an environment where money was scarce, unsafe, or tied to loss.

This book is not about blaming yourself for those patterns. It is about honoring them for what they were—acts of resilience—and learning how to release the ways they sabotage you now. Through reflective practices, guided exercises, and psycho-spiritual insights, you will learn to recognize the unseen contracts you made with struggle, fear, and scarcity. You will uncover how guilt, shame, and imposter syndrome weave themselves into your financial story, and you will be given tools to rewrite those threads with sovereignty and self-compassion.

Our approach is secular and elemental, drawing from universal cycles of nature and, where fitting, pagan-inspired symbolism of roots, growth, and transformation. Just as a tree cannot flourish while strangled by old vines, you cannot thrive if the past keeps tightening around your present. Here, you are invited to gently untangle those vines—not to sever your connection to your roots, but to allow them to nourish you instead of bind you.

I Grew Up Poor and Now I Sabotage My Success is more than a manual for money. It is a mirror, showing you how trauma lingers in prosperity, and a lantern, guiding you toward healing the inner conflicts that keep you from fully embracing your own wealth and worth. This journey is not about erasing where you came from—it is about finally stepping into the life you have worked so hard to build, free from the sabotage of inherited fear.

Chapter 1: Survivor's Guilt — Emotional Residue from Poverty

Escaping poverty is rarely a clean break. The body remembers hunger, the mind recalls nights of scarcity, and the heart clings to the weight of family who never escaped. Survivor's guilt emerges in this tension—when prosperity feels like betrayal, and success awakens sorrow rather than joy.

Growing up poor wires you to survive, not to thrive. You learn to stretch, to sacrifice, to settle. When you finally rise beyond those conditions, a haunting question lingers: *Why me?* You may feel that by earning more, achieving more, or living more fully, you are somehow abandoning those who remain in struggle. This unspoken loyalty keeps you tethered to the old identity of "the poor one," even as your external reality changes.

Survivor's guilt manifests in subtle ways:

- You downplay your achievements to avoid making others feel "less than."
- You self-sabotage by procrastinating, overspending, or undercharging.
- You feel uneasy around family or friends who accuse you of "forgetting where you came from."
- You fear that success will cost you love, belonging, or acceptance.

This chapter offers you a pathway to honor where you came from without carrying its weight as a permanent curse. Through meditation, affirmations, and journaling, you will learn to separate compassion from guilt and create space for authentic growth.

Meditation: Releasing the Old Story

Find a quiet place where you will not be interrupted. Sit or lie comfortably, closing your eyes. Breathe deeply, letting each exhale soften your chest and shoulders.

Visualize yourself standing in two worlds: behind you, the shadowed landscape of your past poverty—small rooms, empty plates, tired faces; before you, a bright horizon of abundance, possibility, and stability.

Imagine a cord tying you to the past. This cord is made of love, loyalty, and unspoken promises. Place your hands over your heart and say:

"I honor those who shaped me. I carry their resilience, not their chains."

Now, in your mind's eye, transform the cord into roots. See them anchoring you—not in shame, but in nourishment. Feel energy rising from the soil into your body. With every breath, the old story feeds your strength rather than drains you. Rest in this vision for several minutes, allowing gratitude to replace guilt.

Affirmations for Healing Survivor's Guilt

Repeat these daily, either aloud or silently, preferably in the morning and before sleep:

1. *I honor my past, but I am not bound by it.*
2. *My success does not diminish others; it creates possibility.*
3. *Wealth and worth are natural extensions of my resilience.*
4. *I allow myself to thrive without apology or guilt.*
5. *By healing myself, I help heal the lineage of poverty I came from.*

Journal Prompts

Use these prompts to uncover hidden layers of survivor's guilt and begin to release them:

1. When I think about being more successful than my family or community, what emotions arise in me?
2. Do I equate having more with abandoning those I love? If so, why?
3. What stories did I hear about "rich people" growing up, and how do they shape my current beliefs?
4. How would my life look if I celebrated my success as an act of generational healing, rather than betrayal?
5. Write a letter to your younger self, reminding them that it is safe to succeed, and that you are carrying their dreams forward—not leaving them behind.

Closing Reflection

Survivor's guilt is not proof that you are unworthy of success—it is proof that you care deeply about belonging. The task is not to erase this care but to redirect it. By reframing success as a continuation of your family's resilience, you transform guilt into gratitude. You are not betraying your roots—you are nourishing them by thriving.

Chapter 2: Unconscious Loyalty to the Struggle

The human spirit craves belonging as much as it craves food, water, or shelter. When you grow up poor, struggle itself can become the currency of connection. The shared hardship—the whispered jokes about "making do," the quiet heroics of stretching meals, the pride of endurance—creates an unspoken bond. It tells you: *You are one of us. We survive together.*

But when your life begins to change, that bond can turn into an invisible chain. Without realizing it, you may remain loyal to the struggle itself, afraid that breaking free means losing love, identity, or community. This "unconscious loyalty" is not chosen deliberately; it's inherited. It's in the body language of your parents, the phrases repeated at the dinner table, the sighs that told you not to dream too big.

Signs of Unconscious Loyalty

- You hesitate to raise your prices or ask for a raise because you "don't want to seem greedy."
- You feel anxious when life gets easier, as if waiting for punishment.
- You bond with others by commiserating about problems rather than celebrating wins.
- You avoid opportunities that could distance you from your community, even if they could uplift you.

The truth is, staying small does not honor your lineage—it repeats its wounds. True loyalty is not to struggle but to survival. And survival, at its highest form, is the freedom to thrive.

Meditation: Meeting the Spirit of Struggle

Find a comfortable position, close your eyes, and breathe slowly. Imagine the "Spirit of Struggle" standing before you—not as an enemy, but as a guardian who once protected you. Perhaps it appears as a weary ancestor, or as a knot of tangled roots, or even as a shadowy figure with watchful eyes.

Greet this spirit and say silently:

"I see you. You taught me how to endure. You kept me alive. But now I choose to live beyond endurance."

Visualize the spirit smiling, then stepping aside, opening a path. Walk through that path, carrying gratitude but leaving the heaviness behind.

Affirmations for Releasing False Loyalty

Speak these daily, especially before moments where guilt or fear about "having more" may arise:

1. *I do not betray my roots by thriving—I honor them.*
2. *My ancestors wanted survival; I transform it into prosperity.*
3. *Struggle was my teacher, but it is not my destiny.*
4. *I belong to love, not to suffering.*
5. *My loyalty is to growth, freedom, and life itself.*

Journal Prompts

Use these to uncover where unconscious loyalty still binds you:

1. Who in my life would feel threatened if I fully stepped into abundance, and why?
2. What phrases about money or struggle echo in my mind from childhood? ("Money doesn't grow on trees," "People like us don't...")
3. In what ways do I *shrink myself* to maintain closeness with others?
4. Imagine a future where you thrive and your family or community is proud instead of resentful—what would need to shift for that to feel safe?
5. Write a dialogue between yourself and the "Spirit of Struggle." What does it say? How do you respond?

Closing Reflection

Unconscious loyalty convinces you that hardship is home and ease is betrayal. But the deeper truth is this: every person who came before you wanted more for you. They may not have known how to reach it, but they dreamed it nonetheless. To thrive is not to abandon them—it is to complete their unfinished prayers for freedom.

You are not leaving them behind. You are carrying their story into a brighter chapter.

Chapter 3: The Saboteur Archetype Within

Every human psyche carries archetypes—patterns of behavior, images, and voices that rise from deep within the unconscious. Some archetypes empower us: the Nurturer, the Creator, the Healer. Others protect us, though their methods may seem destructive. The **Saboteur** is one of these.

The Saboteur is not your enemy. It is the part of you that whispers, *"Don't risk it. Don't outshine. Don't go too far."* Its purpose is survival. It formed when you were young, watching your caregivers struggle with bills, hearing the weight in their voices, or learning that ambition could spark ridicule or disappointment. The Saboteur's job is to keep you safe—even if that means keeping you small.

But the strategies that once shielded you now work against you. The Saboteur shows up as procrastination, overspending, "forgetting" important deadlines, self-doubt before opportunities, or even creating conflict in relationships when things start going well. These are not random mistakes; they are rituals of protection, carried out by an inner guardian who does not yet know you are safe.

Recognizing the Saboteur

The Saboteur archetype has many disguises. You may notice it in these behaviors:

- Starting strong on a project but abandoning it just before completion.
- Feeling anxious after good news, as if waiting for the other shoe to drop.
- Creating arguments or crises during stable times.
- Spending money impulsively after earning it, as though rejecting success.
- Turning down opportunities with excuses like "I'm not ready" or "It's not for people like me."

Each of these is a coded act of loyalty to your past conditions. The Saboteur is trying to protect the younger you who feared failure, loss, or rejection.

Meditation: Facing the Inner Saboteur

Find a quiet space. Breathe deeply, letting your body grow heavy and still.

Visualize yourself in a dimly lit room. Across from you sits a figure—the Saboteur. Notice its form. Perhaps it looks like a nervous child, a stern elder, or a shadow with restless hands. Approach gently.

Say to this figure:

"I see you. I know you are trying to protect me. But I am no longer in danger. I can succeed and still be safe."

As you speak, imagine placing your hand over your heart, sending warmth toward the Saboteur. Watch as its posture softens, its shadow shrinks, or its form transforms into something less threatening. End the meditation by thanking this archetype for its service and assuring it that you will take the lead now.

Affirmations for Transforming the Saboteur

1. *My fear of success is a relic of the past, not my truth today.*
2. *I choose to complete what I begin, with joy and courage.*
3. *Safety and success can exist together in my life.*
4. *I am the author of my story, not the victim of my patterns.*
5. *The part of me that once sabotaged now supports my growth.*

Journal Prompts

1. When do I notice myself "pulling the brake" on success? Describe recent examples.
2. What does my Saboteur look, sound, or feel like? How does it show up in my daily life?
3. What is my Saboteur trying to protect me from? Failure? Rejection? Abandonment?
4. If I could thank my Saboteur for keeping me alive, what would I say?
5. Write a new agreement with your Saboteur, inviting it to become an Ally instead of an Adversary.

Closing Reflection

The Saboteur is not a villain. It is a wounded protector, born in scarcity and fear. By meeting it with compassion, you disarm its power. By giving it a new role—as a guardian of discernment rather than destruction—you reclaim the energy it once drained.

Healing is not about destroying parts of yourself; it is about integration. When you transform the Saboteur, you no longer live at war with yourself. Instead, every part of you begins to row in the same direction—toward the life of safety, abundance, and wholeness you have long deserved.

Chapter 4: Why Joy Feels Unsafe

For those who grew up in poverty, joy can feel like a dangerous luxury. When resources were scarce, moments of pleasure were often fleeting, fragile, or quickly punished. Perhaps you remember a parent saying, *"Don't get too excited—things never last."* Or maybe you recall the sting of a celebration cut short by an unexpected bill, eviction notice, or argument.

Your nervous system learned to associate joy not with safety, but with threat. Joy became the calm before the storm, the brief sunlight that always seemed to invite rain. As adults, this conditioning lingers. You may find yourself shrinking from good news, dismissing compliments, or sabotaging moments of happiness before they can be "taken away."

The Roots of Unsafe Joy

- **Conditional Permission:** In many low-resource households, joy was only acceptable when earned through sacrifice. Pleasure without suffering first was seen as indulgence.
- **Fear of Loss:** When life taught you that good things vanish, it becomes easier to preemptively dim joy than risk devastation when it's gone.
- **Inherited Vigilance:** Families who lived in constant struggle often taught children to stay alert, not relaxed. Joy required letting your guard down, which could feel unsafe.
- **Community Loyalty:** Sometimes, joy feels like betrayal when others around you are still struggling. Smiling too brightly feels like leaving others in the dark.

Signs That Joy Feels Unsafe

- You feel anxious when things are going well, as if disaster is inevitable.
- You minimize or "explain away" your happiness.
- You rush through celebrations instead of savoring them.
- You feel guilty when spending money on things that bring pleasure.
- You "wait for the catch" whenever good fortune arrives.

Meditation: Sitting in the Flame of Joy

Close your eyes and bring to mind a memory of joy, no matter how small—a meal you enjoyed, laughter with a friend, the warmth of sunlight. Allow that moment to expand in your body. Notice where the joy rests—in your chest, stomach, or face.

As you breathe, picture this joy as a golden flame. At first, the flame flickers nervously, threatened by winds of fear. Place your hands over your heart and whisper:

"Joy is safe here. Joy is allowed to live in me."

With every breath, imagine shielding the flame with your hands until it steadies. Let it grow stronger, filling your body with light. End by affirming:

"The storm has passed. I am safe to feel joy."

Affirmations for Safe Joy

1. *It is safe for me to feel joy without fear of loss.*
2. *Joy is nourishment, not indulgence.*
3. *My happiness does not harm others; it radiates possibility.*
4. *I am worthy of delight in both small and great forms.*
5. *I allow myself to celebrate fully, without apology.*

Journal Prompts

1. Recall a childhood moment when joy was interrupted. How has that memory shaped the way you feel about happiness now?
2. What emotions surface when something goes well for you? Excitement? Fear? Suspicion?
3. Do I equate happiness with danger? If so, when did I first learn this?
4. What would it look like to fully celebrate a recent success without minimizing it?
5. Write a letter to your younger self, telling them that joy is no longer dangerous—that you are safe now to receive it fully.

Closing Reflection

Joy is not a trick, a trap, or a fleeting accident—it is your birthright. Poverty may have taught you that joy was fragile, that laughter would summon pain, or that pleasure was undeserved. But those were survival lessons, not eternal truths.

When you choose to embrace joy without fear, you re-train your nervous system and spirit. You show yourself that happiness does not have to vanish, and even if life brings challenges, joy can coexist alongside them. True wealth is not only measured in money—it is measured in your capacity to feel safe while smiling, laughing, and celebrating the life you have fought to create.

Chapter 5: Fear of Visibility and Success

Success often brings a spotlight, and for those who grew up poor, that spotlight can feel more like a weapon than a gift. Visibility exposes you to judgment, envy, and expectations. When you were raised in environments where standing out was unsafe—whether because it drew criticism, gossip, or even danger—the idea of being seen in your success can awaken primal fear.

This fear is not irrational. In poverty, being visible often meant being vulnerable. Perhaps neighbors whispered about the one family who suddenly "had money." Perhaps teachers dismissed your talents because they assumed your background meant you wouldn't go far. Maybe family members shamed you for wanting "too much." Over time, your subconscious linked success with exposure—and exposure with harm.

So even as you dream of wealth, your body resists. You may delay launching projects, hide your achievements, or sabotage growth, believing on some level that staying small keeps you safe.

The Roots of Fear of Visibility

- **Cultural Beliefs:** In many families, humility is demanded, and ambition is mistaken for arrogance. Being "too visible" risks rejection.
- **Survival Programming:** Growing up poor often meant blending in, not attracting attention. Visibility felt dangerous when resources were scarce.
- **Community Dynamics:** Success can cause tension with peers or relatives, who may feel left behind. To avoid conflict, you unconsciously hide your light.
- **Internalized Shame:** Poverty often imprints the message that you are "less than." When success shines a light, that shame whispers, *"They'll see I'm a fraud."*

Signs of Fear of Visibility

- Avoiding leadership opportunities or promotions.
- Downplaying accomplishments when praised.
- Hesitating to share creative work, fearing judgment.
- Worrying that wealth will alienate you from loved ones.
- Feeling exposed or anxious when others notice your success.

Meditation: Stepping Into the Circle of Light

Close your eyes and imagine yourself standing in a dark forest. Above you, a single circle of light shines down, illuminating the ground.

You hesitate at the edge, heart racing. Then, with each breath, imagine your feet carrying you forward until you stand in the center of the light. At first, you feel naked, judged, unsafe. But slowly, you notice the warmth of the light on your skin, the way it supports you rather than burns you.

Whisper to yourself:

"I am safe to be seen. My visibility is not a threat—it is a beacon."

See the forest around you transform—not with hostile eyes, but with faces smiling, inspired by your courage to step forward. Stay here until your body feels calmer in the light, training your nervous system to recognize visibility as safety.

Affirmations for Safe Success

1. *It is safe for me to be visible in my success.*
2. *My light inspires rather than threatens others.*
3. *Being seen does not endanger me—it empowers me.*
4. *I no longer shrink to stay small. I expand with trust.*
5. *I am worthy of recognition, celebration, and abundance.*

Journal Prompts

1. Recall a time when you were shamed or criticized for standing out. How has that memory shaped your comfort with success?
2. What fears arise when you imagine being truly visible—on stage, online, or in your community?
3. Who in your life might react negatively to your success, and what story does that reinforce?
4. What would it mean to reframe visibility as leadership rather than exposure?
5. Write a letter from your future self who is successful, visible, and safe. What do they tell you about this journey?

Closing Reflection

Visibility is not betrayal. It is not arrogance. It is not danger. It is your birthright to be fully expressed, fully seen, and fully celebrated. Poverty may have taught you to hide, to blend, to protect yourself by being invisible. But that camouflage no longer serves you.

When you step into the light, you don't just liberate yourself—you hold a lantern for others still walking in the dark. Your visibility is not selfish; it is service. Success does not exile you from your roots—it illuminates them, showing what is possible when survival transforms into sovereignty.

Chapter 6: Rewriting Your Success Narrative

Every life is shaped by stories. Some are spoken aloud—family sayings, community proverbs, generational warnings. Others live quietly inside you, whispered by memory and reinforced by repetition. These narratives form the framework through which you interpret wealth, worth, and success.

If you grew up poor, those stories often sounded like:

- *"People like us don't get rich."*
- *"Money doesn't grow on trees."*
- *"Don't aim too high—you'll only get hurt."*
- *"Rich people are selfish, greedy, or corrupt."*

These were not random phrases; they were survival scripts. They shielded you from disappointment, gave meaning to struggle, and created a sense of shared identity. But today, those scripts no longer protect you—they sabotage you. Rewriting your success narrative is not about erasing your past. It is about updating the story so that it aligns with who you are becoming, not who you were forced to be.

Why Narrative Matters

The subconscious mind does not operate by logic alone—it responds to story, symbolism, and repetition. If your inner story tells you that wealth is dangerous, your body will resist it no matter how hard you work. If your inner story tells you that abundance is betrayal, you will unconsciously shrink every time you rise.

To truly heal money sabotage, you must become the author of your narrative. You must write a story where success is safe, wealth is natural, and prosperity is part of your lineage rather than a break from it.

Steps to Rewriting Your Success Narrative

1. **Identify the Old Script**
   Write down the money stories you grew up hearing. Notice which ones you still repeat, consciously or unconsciously.
2. **Name the Origin**
   Ask: *Who did I learn this from?* Often, these scripts come from parents, grandparents, or communities doing the best they could. Naming the origin helps you see the story as inherited, not absolute truth.
3. **Challenge the Script**
   Ask: *Is this always true? Does this belief serve me now?* Even if it kept you safe as a child, you are free to outgrow it as an adult.
4. **Craft the New Narrative**
   Replace limiting scripts with expansive ones. For example:
   - Old: *"Money changes people."*
   - New: *"Money reveals my generosity and freedom."*
   - Old: *"Success will isolate me."*
   - New: *"Success connects me with people who celebrate my growth."*

5.Embody the New Story

Stories stick when they are practiced. Speak your new narrative aloud. Write it down daily. Enact it with small, symbolic actions—like celebrating a win instead of downplaying it.

Meditation: The Story Weaver

Close your eyes and imagine sitting at a loom. In one hand, you hold threads of your old narrative—frayed, dark, and tangled. In the other hand, you hold golden threads of your new story—bright, smooth, and resilient.

Begin weaving. With each inhale, place an old thread into the tapestry and let it dissolve. With each exhale, weave a golden thread into place, watching the fabric of your life transform before your eyes.

Whisper to yourself:

"I am the author of my story. I weave a narrative of success, safety, and abundance."

Sit in this vision until you feel the tapestry forming, vibrant and whole.

Affirmations for Narrative Renewal

1. *I release inherited stories that no longer serve me.*
2. *I am free to write a new chapter of success and prosperity.*
3. *My wealth narrative is one of safety, joy, and connection.*
4. *I honor my roots while creating a story of growth beyond them.*
5. *I am the storyteller of my destiny, not the victim of my past.*

Journal Prompts

1. What are three money or success sayings I heard often as a child? How have they shaped my choices?
2. Which of those stories no longer reflect my truth?
3. Write a paragraph beginning with: *"My new story about wealth and success is..."*
4. Imagine your future self ten years from now, fully living your new narrative. What does their life look like?
5. How can I practice living my new story this week—in one small, tangible way?

Closing Reflection

Rewriting your success narrative is not about denying the struggles of your past. It is about acknowledging them while refusing to let them dictate your future. You are both the child who survived scarcity and the adult who creates abundance.

When you reclaim authorship, you no longer repeat the scripts of poverty—you compose a new legacy. Your wealth becomes not an accident, not a betrayal, but the natural continuation of your courage.

Chapter 7: The Comfort of Chaos

For many who grew up poor, chaos was the air you breathed. Bills came late. Power shut-offs arrived without warning. Arguments erupted without rhythm. The ground beneath you was never steady. In that environment, chaos became normal—so normal, in fact, that peace can feel foreign, even threatening.

When your nervous system adapts to unpredictability, calm doesn't feel safe; it feels suspicious. If things are too quiet, you wait for the storm. If life flows too easily, you unconsciously stir the waters. This attachment to instability is not weakness—it's a survival imprint. Chaos was once proof that you were still alive, still adapting, still braced for the next hit.

But now, as an adult, this loyalty to chaos sabotages your growth. Stability—financial, emotional, relational—requires learning to tolerate stillness. To sit with safety without mistaking it for danger.

Why Chaos Feels Like Home

- **Survival Training:** Growing up in poverty taught you that vigilance was safety. Chaos sharpened your reflexes; calm dulled them.
- **Emotional Bonding:** Families often bond during crisis. If love was most present during emergencies, part of you believes chaos is the only way to stay connected.
- **Identity Attachment:** When hardship defines your story, you may fear losing yourself if life becomes too easy.
- **Unprocessed Trauma:** The body associates unpredictability with familiarity. Predictability can feel unnatural, even boring, to a nervous system wired for survival.

Signs You Are Attached to Chaos

- You feel restless or anxious during calm periods.
- You unconsciously overspend just when finances stabilize.
- You create conflict in relationships during peaceful stretches.
- You procrastinate until a crisis forces you to act.
- You feel more alive in survival mode than in steady growth.

Meditation: Finding Stillness in the River

Sit in a comfortable position and close your eyes. Imagine a rushing river, loud and wild. This river represents the chaos you once lived in. Step gently onto a boat and let it carry you downstream.

After some time, the river widens and calms. The waters turn smooth, the noise fades. At first, your body tenses, waiting for the rapids to return. Place your hand on your heart and whisper:

"Calm is safe. Peace nourishes me. Stillness is not danger—it is freedom."

Allow yourself to float, noticing the beauty of the smooth water. Imagine your body syncing with the river's rhythm, teaching your nervous system to rest in serenity.

Affirmations for Embracing Stability

1. *I am safe in stillness.*
2. *Stability is not weakness—it is strength.*
3. *Peace is not boring; it is the soil where growth takes root.*
4. *I no longer need chaos to feel alive.*
5. *Calm supports me as much as resilience once did.*

Journal Prompts

1. When has peace or calm felt "wrong" or unsafe to me? Describe the moment.
2. How did my family respond to periods of calm? Did they celebrate it, or did tension build until chaos returned?
3. In what ways do I unconsciously recreate instability in my finances, work, or relationships?
4. What would it mean to redefine calm as abundance rather than emptiness?
5. Write a vision of your ideal life where peace, predictability, and success coexist—and where you feel at home in that life.

Closing Reflection

Chaos was once your compass. It guided your survival, kept you vigilant, and gave shape to your days. But you are no longer trapped in survival. You have the power to step into stability, to recognize peace as the fertile ground of prosperity rather than a prelude to disaster.

The comfort of chaos is not true comfort. It is a ghost of the past, asking you to repeat what you no longer need. By retraining your body and spirit to embrace calm, you choose a new rhythm—one where success and safety do not collapse into chaos, but stand together as allies.

Chapter 8: Redefining Wealth Beyond Money

When you grow up poor, money often becomes the sole definition of wealth. It is the measure of safety, freedom, and possibility. Yet, paradoxically, this narrow view can also trap you. If wealth equals only dollars in the bank, then every financial dip feels like collapse, every expense like failure, and every success like it could be snatched away.

To heal from poverty's shadow, you must expand your definition of wealth. True abundance is multi-dimensional. It is not just what you earn, but how you live. It is not only income, but also inner richness—energy, creativity, love, and time. Money is important, but it is not the only currency of a wealthy life.

The Hidden Currencies of Abundance

1. **Time** – Poverty teaches you that time must always be traded for survival. True wealth means reclaiming hours for rest, creativity, and pleasure without guilt.
2. **Health** – Energy, vitality, and well-being are forms of wealth often overlooked until they are lost. Success includes tending to your body as a sacred resource.
3. **Relationships** – Genuine connection, trust, and love cannot be bought. They are wealth in its purest form.
4. **Freedom** – The ability to choose your path, speak your truth, and move without fear is a currency that transcends money.
5. **Joy** – Laughter, creativity, and delight are signs of abundance. Joy is not an accessory to wealth—it is wealth.
6. **Legacy** – Impact, contribution, and generational healing are currencies that ripple beyond your own life.

Why Expanding Wealth Heals Sabotage

When money is your only definition of success, every fear, doubt, and failure attaches itself to it. By redefining wealth, you unhook prosperity from fragility. You allow yourself to celebrate abundance even when your bank balance shifts. You reclaim agency by realizing:

- A slow day at work does not mean you are worthless—you may have gained rest, which is wealth.
- An unexpected expense does not erase your abundance—you still carry relationships, health, creativity, and freedom.
- A temporary setback does not define you—you are still moving forward in dimensions beyond money.

This shift disarms sabotage because it reframes success not as a fragile number, but as a living ecosystem of abundance.

Meditation: Gathering Your Currencies

Close your eyes. Imagine standing before a great table. On this table are bowls, each filled with a different currency of wealth: time, health, relationships, freedom, joy, legacy, and money.

Approach each bowl in turn. Place your hands over it and whisper:
"I claim this wealth. It belongs to me as much as money does."

Notice which bowl feels full, and which feels neglected. Spend a few breaths pouring energy into the neglected bowls, balancing your wealth across all dimensions. End by placing your hand on the bowl of money and affirm:
"Money is one of many forms of my abundance."

Affirmations for Expanded Wealth

1. *I am wealthy in more ways than money alone.*
2. *Time, health, joy, and love are currencies I honor.*
3. *I release the belief that money is my only measure of worth.*
4. *Every day, I grow richer in multiple dimensions of life.*
5. *True abundance flows through me and around me in many forms.*

Journal Prompts

1. How did my upbringing shape my definition of wealth? Was it only tied to money, or were other forms acknowledged?
2. Which non-monetary currencies of wealth do I already hold in abundance?
3. Which of these currencies (time, health, relationships, freedom, joy, legacy) do I want to expand right now?
4. How does redefining wealth help me feel safer, calmer, or more fulfilled in moments of financial stress?
5. Write a vision of your life as abundantly wealthy across all dimensions—not just money.

Closing Reflection

Money is a vital part of abundance, but it is not the whole story. By expanding your definition of wealth, you loosen poverty's grip on your psyche. You learn to honor time as treasure, joy as inheritance, love as capital, and freedom as fortune.

When you live by this expanded definition, you no longer measure success by a fragile balance sheet—you measure it by the richness of your days. In this way, you build a foundation that no setback can erase. Wealth becomes not only what you own, but who you are becoming.

Chapter 9: Belonging Without Struggle

One of the deepest wounds of poverty is the belief that belonging requires suffering. In households and communities where survival was constant, struggle became the glue that bound people together. Complaining about bills, stretching meals, or joking about scarcity became shared rituals. It was not just hardship—it was identity, culture, and belonging.

So when you rise into success, part of you may feel like an outsider. You may fear that others will think you've "changed" or that you no longer understand their lives. You may even sabotage yourself to stay connected, shrinking your joy so others don't feel abandoned. The unconscious story says: *If I stop struggling, I stop belonging.*

But true belonging is not built on suffering. It is built on authenticity, love, and shared humanity. To thrive without struggle, you must reframe connection as something deeper than pain.

The Roots of Belonging Through Struggle

- **Shared Identity:** Families often forged unity in hardship—leaning on each other during crises more than in calm.
- **Inherited Loyalty:** You may believe that suffering with others proves love, while success distances you.
- **Fear of Rejection:** Thriving can trigger guilt if you believe others will envy or resent you.
- **Internalized Stories:** Growing up, you may have heard phrases like, *"Don't forget where you came from,"* or *"People like us don't..."* These created unspoken contracts between struggle and loyalty.

Signs You Equate Belonging with Struggle

- Feeling uneasy celebrating success around family or friends.
- Downplaying achievements so others don't feel "left behind."
- Sabotaging prosperity when it threatens to set you apart.
- Feeling most connected when consoling others in difficulty, not when sharing joy.
- Believing comfort means disconnection.

Meditation: Finding Belonging in the Circle of Abundance

Sit in stillness and close your eyes. Imagine a circle of people you love—family, friends, ancestors. At first, each holds a heavy stone, symbolizing struggle. The weight keeps the circle together.

Now, in your vision, imagine each stone dissolving into light. The circle does not break. Instead, the light flows between you all, weaving threads of connection made of joy, love, and shared possibility.

Whisper:

"I belong through love, not through suffering. Connection does not require struggle."

See the circle glow brighter, whole without heaviness. Rest in this image until you feel warmth in your body.

Affirmations for Belonging in Success

1. *I do not need to suffer to prove my love or loyalty.*
2. *I am worthy of belonging even in joy and abundance.*
3. *Those who love me truly celebrate my growth.*
4. *I carry my roots with me as I rise—they do not keep me small.*
5. *Connection is built on authenticity, not hardship.*

Journal Prompts

1. What messages did I hear about "forgetting where you came from"? How have they shaped my beliefs about success?
2. In what ways have I minimized or hidden my prosperity to maintain belonging?
3. Who in my life can I fully share joy and abundance with, without fear of rejection?
4. What would it look like to create relationships where thriving, not suffering, is the bond?
5. Write a letter to yourself affirming: *"I belong as I succeed. My success expands connection, not diminishes it."*

Closing Reflection

Belonging rooted in struggle is fragile. It chains love to hardship and makes prosperity feel like betrayal. But belonging rooted in authenticity is unbreakable. It allows you to thrive and remain connected, because love is not measured by how much you suffer—it is measured by how true you are.

When you choose to belong without struggle, you rewrite the script for yourself and for those who come after you. You become proof that family, love, and community do not need pain as glue—they can be bound by joy, possibility, and shared abundance.

Chapter 10: Anchoring Success Into Your Body

Success is not only a mental or financial journey—it is a full-bodied experience. When you grew up poor, your nervous system learned to carry stress in your muscles, tension in your breath, and vigilance in your bones. Even as your outer circumstances change, your body may still live as though scarcity is always around the corner.

Anchoring success means teaching your body that prosperity is safe, stable, and sustainable. It means shifting abundance from a fragile thought into a lived sensation you can carry daily. Without embodiment, success remains fragile; with it, success becomes rooted like a tree with deep, unshakable roots.

Why the Body Holds Poverty's Ghosts

- **Hypervigilance:** Growing up poor often trains your nervous system to anticipate crisis, making relaxation feel dangerous.
- **Tension Storage:** Chronic stress imprints itself in the shoulders, jaw, or stomach, creating physical echoes of scarcity.
- **Distrust of Calm:** Stillness may trigger unease because the body associates it with waiting for disaster.
- **Emotional Imprints:** Fear, shame, or guilt about money often surface as tightness, fatigue, or illness.

Practices for Anchoring Success

1. **Breathwork for Abundance**
   Sit upright. Inhale deeply, imagining you are drawing in golden light. Hold for four counts. Exhale slowly, releasing tension with the thought: *"I am safe to hold success."* Repeat for 3–5 minutes.
2. **Grounding Ritual**
   Stand barefoot on the floor or earth. Visualize roots extending from your feet deep into the ground. As you breathe, imagine pulling stability upward, anchoring abundance into your legs, hips, and core.
3. **Somatic Celebration**
   Each time you experience a success—big or small—pause. Instead of rushing on, place your hand on your chest and say aloud: *"This belongs to me."* Smile, stretch, or even dance. Let your body register joy so success feels embodied, not abstract.

Meditation: Rooting Prosperity

Close your eyes and imagine yourself as a great tree. Each breath draws nourishment from the soil, filling your trunk with strength. Around you, branches spread, heavy with fruit. Whisper:

"I am rooted. My success is not fleeting. I thrive with stability."

Stay in this vision until your body feels heavier, grounded, and calm—proof that you can hold abundance without fear.

Affirmations for Embodied Success

1. *My body is a safe home for abundance.*
2. *Success lives in me as breath, rhythm, and strength.*
3. *I no longer brace for collapse—I root into stability.*
4. *Every cell of my body welcomes prosperity.*
5. *I thrive with ease, calm, and grounded joy.*

Journal Prompts

1. Where in my body do I feel poverty's residue—tightness, pain, or fatigue?
2. How does my body react when I receive money, praise, or success?
3. What practices (movement, breath, rituals) help me feel grounded in abundance?
4. How can I create daily rituals that anchor prosperity into my body?
5. Write a vision of your life where success feels steady in your body—not fragile or fleeting.

Closing Reflection

Anchoring success into your body frees you from the cycle of rise and sabotage. Instead of fearing collapse, you learn to rest in prosperity as a natural state. Poverty once lived in your body as tension; abundance can live there now as calm, breath, and rooted joy.

You are not only changing your mind—you are retraining your whole being to feel at home in success.

Appendix A: Success-Sabotage Inventory Sheet

A Practical Tool for Identifying Patterns That Hold You Back

The purpose of this inventory is to help you clearly see how unconscious sabotage shows up in your life. Awareness is the first step toward transformation. By listing patterns, emotions, and triggers, you begin to map the hidden terrain of self-sabotage—and from there, you can make conscious choices to respond differently.

Instructions for Use

1. **Set the Scene:** Find a quiet, reflective space. Have a notebook or printed version of this sheet ready.
2. **Be Honest:** Write without judgment. The goal is to observe, not to criticize.
3. **Look for Patterns:** The more examples you record, the easier it is to notice recurring themes.
4. **Return Regularly:** This inventory isn't one-and-done. Revisit monthly or quarterly as new insights emerge.

Part I: Identifying Sabotage Behaviors

Prompt: List the ways you notice yourself *blocking, delaying, or minimizing* your own success. Examples are provided to spark ideas.

Sabotage Behavior	When It Shows Up	What I Tell Myself	Possible Root Belief
Procrastination (e.g., delaying big projects)	Before deadlines	"I'm not ready yet."	Fear of failure / success
Overspending	After payday	"I deserve this now."	Fear of holding money
Downplaying accomplishments	When praised	"It's not a big deal."	Fear of being envied or rejected
Conflict creation	During calm	"Something feels off."	Loyalty to chaos
Avoiding opportunities	When invited to grow	"It's not for people like me."	Poverty identity

(Add rows for your own behaviors.)

Part II: Emotional Triggers

Prompt: What emotions often precede or follow sabotage behaviors?

- Fear of failure
- Fear of success
- Guilt (for having more than others)
- Shame (of not deserving abundance)
- Anxiety (when things go too well)
- Loneliness (believing success isolates me)

(Circle or highlight the ones that resonate most, and write notes about when you feel them.)

Part III: Situations That Activate Sabotage

Prompt: Identify situations where sabotage is most likely to appear.

- Around family who expect me to "stay the same."
- When I receive money or recognition.
- During moments of calm or stability.
- When opportunities require me to be visible.
- When I begin to feel joy.

(List additional personal triggers.)

Part IV: Reframing Statement

For each sabotage behavior, write a *new supportive belief* that can take its place.

Example:

- Old Behavior: Procrastination.
- Root Belief: "If I succeed, I'll be judged."
- Reframing Statement: *"I am safe to succeed, and my work deserves completion."*

Part V: Success-Supporting Practices

List rituals, habits, or actions that help you stay aligned when sabotage patterns arise.

- Deep breathing before responding to fear.
- Journaling to name the trigger.
- Grounding rituals (barefoot on earth, hand on heart).
- Repeating affirmations from earlier chapters.
- Reaching out to a supportive friend, mentor, or group.

Closing Reflection

This inventory sheet is not a scorecard of your failures—it is a map of your resilience. Each behavior you list once protected you. Each trigger points to a story waiting to be rewritten. By recording and reflecting, you take ownership of your patterns rather than letting them silently steer your life.

Remember: sabotage is not proof that you are broken. It is proof that you are healing—ready to upgrade old survival strategies into new ways of thriving.

Appendix B: Emotional Success Anchoring Exercise

A Daily Ritual for Rooting Success into Body and Spirit

Success is not just achieved—it must be felt. For those who grew up poor, success can remain fragile if it lives only in the mind. You may know you're doing well, but your body still braces for collapse. Anchoring is a way of teaching your nervous system and emotions that prosperity is safe, real, and lasting.

This exercise creates a bridge between thought, body, and feeling. By repeating it consistently, you train yourself to embody abundance until it becomes your natural state.

Preparation

- Choose a quiet space where you feel secure.
- Have a journal or notebook nearby for reflection.
- Select a small object (stone, coin, pendant, or talisman) that will serve as your **anchor object**—a physical reminder of success.

Step 1: Recall a Moment of Success

Close your eyes. Bring to mind a recent memory when you felt successful. It doesn't need to be grand—it could be finishing a project, paying a bill with ease, or receiving praise. Let the memory sharpen in detail: Where were you? What did you see, hear, and feel?

Breathe into that memory until the emotion of success rises in your body—whether it's warmth in the chest, lightness in the face, or energy in the stomach.

Step 2: Anchor the Feeling in the Body

Place your hand over your heart or stomach. With each inhale, say silently:

"This success belongs to me. I am safe to hold it."

With each exhale, imagine the feeling of success sinking deeper into your muscles, bones, and breath—like roots anchoring into soil.

Repeat for 5–7 breaths.

Step 3: Transfer the Energy to the Anchor Object

Pick up your chosen object. Hold it firmly while recalling the successful feeling. Whisper aloud:

"You carry this memory of abundance. Whenever I touch you, I remember my success."

Visualize the energy flowing from your body into the object, charging it like a battery. From now on, whenever you feel doubt or fear, holding this object will help recall the anchored emotion.

Step 4: Expand the Anchor with Affirmations

Speak the following affirmations slowly, allowing the anchored feeling to grow stronger:

1. *Success feels natural and safe in my body.*
2. *Every breath roots me deeper into abundance.*
3. *I am worthy of joy, prosperity, and stability.*
4. *Success is not fleeting—it lives in me.*
5. *I carry this strength wherever I go.*

Step 5: Journal Reflection

After the exercise, answer these questions:

1. What sensations did I notice in my body when I recalled success?
2. How did the anchor object feel once charged with this energy?
3. What doubts or fears arose, and how did I respond to them?
4. How do I feel now compared to before the exercise?

Write freely—this helps reinforce the practice in both mind and spirit.

Consistency Practice

- **Daily Use:** Practice anchoring for 5–10 minutes each morning or evening.
- **In-the-Moment Use:** Whenever sabotage patterns arise—procrastination, fear, guilt—hold your anchor object, breathe deeply, and recall the feeling of success.
- **Monthly Recharge:** Once a month, repeat the exercise with a new success memory to keep the anchor strong and relevant.

Closing Reflection

Your body has long been trained to expect struggle. Anchoring success retrains it to expect abundance. By linking prosperity to breath, touch, and a physical symbol, you create stability that no financial setback or emotional trigger can undo. Success becomes not only an external achievement, but an internal truth

Appendix C: Journal Prompts

A Toolkit for Self-Reflection and Success Healing

Journaling is one of the most powerful ways to uncover unconscious beliefs, release emotional residue from poverty, and anchor new patterns of success. Writing bypasses the chatter of the mind and draws out truths hidden beneath the surface. This collection of prompts is organized by theme, offering you guidance no matter where you are in your journey.

Section 1: Tracing the Roots of Poverty's Stories

1. What were the first things I learned about money growing up? Who taught me those lessons?
2. How did my family or community talk about "rich people"? What tone or judgment was in those conversations?
3. What role did struggle play in creating closeness in my family?
4. What moments from childhood shaped my view of safety, stability, or lack of it?
5. What sayings or "rules" about money and success still echo in my head today?

Section 2: Uncovering Sabotage Patterns

1. When have I noticed myself pulling back just as things were going well? Describe specific examples.
2. What behaviors do I repeat that delay or block my success? (Procrastination, overspending, self-doubt, etc.)
3. What emotions often come right before I sabotage my progress—fear, guilt, shame, or something else?
4. Do I believe that I must suffer to belong? If so, where did that belief come from?
5. What opportunities have I turned down because they felt “too big” or “not for me”?

Section 3: Healing Guilt and Fear

1. When I imagine having more than my family or friends, what feelings surface?
2. Do I fear success will cause me to lose love or connection? Why?
3. How does joy feel in my body—safe, unsafe, fleeting, suspicious?
4. What's the earliest memory of being shamed for wanting more?
5. How can I reframe success as healing for my lineage, not betrayal of it?

Section 4: Redefining Wealth

1. Aside from money, what currencies of wealth (time, health, joy, relationships, freedom, legacy) do I currently possess?
2. Which of these currencies do I want to grow more of right now?
3. How does redefining wealth beyond money shift the way I measure my success?
4. What small daily practices help me feel abundant, regardless of my bank account?
5. Write a paragraph beginning with: *"My wealth is measured not only in money, but also in..."*

Section 5: Belonging Without Struggle

1. How do I behave differently around people who are still struggling financially?
2. Do I minimize my accomplishments to make others comfortable?
3. Who can I fully share my joy and prosperity with? Who feels unsafe to share it with?
4. How do I want to model success for future generations or my community?
5. Write a letter to yourself affirming: *"I belong as I thrive. My success expands connection."*

Section 6: Anchoring and Integration

1. Where in my body do I feel tension when I think about money or success?
2. What practices (movement, breathwork, ritual) help me feel calm and grounded in prosperity?
3. How can I create daily reminders that success is safe and lasting?
4. What small success can I celebrate today, and how will I anchor it in my body?
5. Write a vision of your life ten years from now where abundance is natural, safe, and joyful.

Tips for Journaling

- **Write Daily, Even Briefly:** Consistency matters more than length.
- **Do Not Edit:** Let the words flow without judgment. Messy truths are valuable.
- **Return Later:** Review old entries after weeks or months—you will notice growth and shifts in perspective.
- **Pair With Rituals:** Light a candle, place your anchor object nearby, or breathe deeply before writing. These actions reinforce your journaling as a sacred practice.

Closing Reflection

Journaling is more than writing—it is ritualized self-listening. Each prompt is an invitation to step into honesty, release inherited patterns, and imagine a life beyond sabotage. Over time, your journal becomes a map of your transformation: the story of how you rewrote poverty's residue into a narrative of belonging, safety, and abundance.

Message from the Author:

I hope you enjoyed this book, I love astrology and knew there was not a book such as this out on the shelf. I love metaphysical items as well. Please check out my other books:

-Life of Government Benefits

-My life of Hell

-My life with Hydrocephalus

-Red Sky

-World Domination:Woman's rule

-World Domination:Woman's Rule 2: The War

-Life and Banishment of Apophis: book 1

-The Kidney Friendly Diet

-The Ultimate Hemp Cookbook

-Creating a Dispensary(legally)

-Cleanliness throughout life: the importance of showering from childhood to adulthood.

-Strong Roots: The Risks of Overcoddling children

-Hemp Horoscopes: Cosmic Insights and Earthly Healing

- Celestial Hemp Navigating the Zodiac: Through the Green Cosmos

-Astrological Hemp: Aligning The Stars with Earth's Ancient Herb

-The Astrological Guide to Hemp: Stars, Signs, and Sacred Leaves

-Green Growth: Innovative Marketing Strategies for your Hemp Products and Dispensary

-Cosmic Cannabis

-Astrological Munchies

-Henry The Hemp

-Zodiacal Roots: The Astrological Soul Of Hemp

- **Green Constellations: Intersection of Hemp and Zodiac**

-Hemp in The Houses: An astrological Adventure Through The Cannabis Galaxy

-Galactic Ganja Guide

Heavenly Hemp
Zodiac Leaves
Doctor Who Astrology
Cannastrology
Stellar Satvias and Cosmic Indicas
Celestial Cannabis: A Zodiac Journey
AstroHerbology: The Sky and The Soil: Volume 1
AstroHerbology:Celestial Cannabis:Volume 2
Cosmic Cannabis Cultivation
The Starry Guide to Herbal Harmony: Volume 1
The Starry Guide to Herbal Harmony: Cannabis Universe: Volume 2
Yugioh Astrology: Astrological Guide to Deck, Duels and more
Nightmare Mansion: Echoes of The Abyss
Nightmare Mansion 2: Legacy of Shadows
Nightmare Mansion 3: Shadows of the Forgotten
Nightmare Mansion 4: Echoes of the Damned
The Life and Banishment of Apophis: Book 2
Nightmare Mansion: Halls of Despair
Healing with Herb: Cannabis and Hydrocephalus
Planetary Pot: Aligning with Astrological Herbs: Volume 1
Fast Track to Freedom: 30 Days to Financial Independence Using AI, Assets, and Agile Hustles
Cosmic Hemp Pathways
How to Become Financially Free in 30 Days: 10,000 Paths to Prosperity
Zodiacal Herbage: Astrological Insights: Volume 1
Nightmare Mansion: Whispers in the Walls
The Daleks Invade Atlantis
Henry the hemp and Hydrocephalus

10X The Kidney Friendly Diet
Cannabis Universe: Adult coloring book

Hemp Astrology: The Healing Power of the Stars

Zodiacal Herbage: Astrological Insights: Cannabis Universe: Volume 2

Planetary Pot: Aligning with Astrological Herbs: Cannabis Universes: Volume 2

Doctor Who: Convergence Protocol – The Replicator War

Nightmare Mansion: Curse of the Blood Moon

The Celestial Stoner: A Guide to the Zodiac

Cosmic Pleasures: Sex Toy Astrology for Every Sign

Hydrocephalus Astrology: Navigating the Stars and Healing Waters

Lapis and the Mischievous Chocolate Bar

Celestial Positions: Sexual Astrology for Every Sign

Apophis's Shadow Work Journal: **:** A Journey of Self-Discovery and Healing

Kinky Cosmos: Sexual Kink Astrology for Every Sign

Digital Cosmos: The Astrological Digimon Compendium

Stellar Seeds: The Cosmic Guide to Growing with Astrology

Apophis's Daily Gratitude Journal

Cat Astrology: Feline Mysteries of the Cosmos

The Cosmic Kama Sutra: An Astrological Guide to Sexual Positions

Unleash Your Potential: A Guided Journal Powered by AI Insights

Whispers of the Enchanted Grove

Cosmic Pleasures: An Astrological Guide to Sexual Kinks

369, 12 Manifestation Journal

Whisper of the nocturne journal(blank journal for writing or drawing)

The Boogey Book

Locked In Reflection: A Chastity Journey Through Locktober

Generating Wealth Quickly:How to Generate $100,000 in 24 Hours

Star Magic: Harness the Power of the Universe

The Flatulence Chronicles: A Fart Journal for Self-Discovery

The Doctor and The Death Moth

Seize the Day: A Personal Seizure Tracking Journal

The Ultimate Boogeyman Safari: A Journey into the Boogie World and Beyond

Whispers of Samhain: 1,000 Spells of Love, Luck, and Lunar Magic: Samhain Spell Book

Apophis's guides:Witch's Spellbook Crafting Guide for Halloween

Frost & Flame: The Enchanted Yule Grimoire of 1000 Winter Spells

The Ultimate Boogey Goo Guide & Spooky Activities for Halloween Fun

Harmony of the Scales: A Libra's Spellcraft for Balance and Beauty

The Enchanted Advent: 36 Days of Christmas Wonders

Nightmare Mansion: The Labyrinth of Screams

Harvest of Enchantment: 1,000 Spells of Gratitude, Love, and Fortune for Thanksgiving

The Boogey Chronicles: A Journal of Nightly Encounters and Shadowy Secrets

The 12 Days of Financial Freedom: A Step-by-Step Christmas Countdown to Transform Your Finances

Sigil of the Eternal Spiral Blank Journal

A Christmas Feast: Timeless Recipes for Every Meal

Holiday Stress-Free Solutions: A Survival Guide to Thriving During the Festive Season

Yu-Gi-Oh! Holiday Gifting Mastery: The Ultimate Guide for Fans and Newcomers Alike

Holiday Harmony: A Hydrocephalus Survival Guide for the Festive Season

Celestial Craft: The Witch's Almanac for 2025 – A Cosmic Guide to Manifestations, Moons, and Mystical Events

Doctor Who: The Toymaker's Winter Wonderland

Tulsa King Unveiled: A Thrilling Guide to Stallone's Mafia Masterpiece

Pendulum Craft: A Complete Guide to Crafting and Using Personalized Divination Tools

Nightmare Mansion: Santa's Eternal Eve

Starlight Noel: A Cosmic Journey through Christmas Mysteries

The Dark Architect: Unlocking the Blueprint of Existence

Surviving the Embrace: The Ultimate Guide to Encounters with The Hugging Molly

The Enchanted Codex: Secrets of the Craft for Witches, Wiccans, and Pagans

Harvest of Gratitude: A Complete Thanksgiving Guide

Yuletide Essentials: A Complete Guide to an Authentic and Magical Christmas

Celestial Smokes: A Cosmic Guide to Cigars and Astrology

Living in Balance: A Comprehensive Survival Guide to Thriving with Diabetes Insipidus

Cosmic Symbiosis: The Venom Zodiac Chronicles

The Cursed Paw of Ambition

Cosmic Symbiosis: The Astrological Venom Journal

Celestial Wonders Unfold: A Stargazer's Guide to the Cosmos (2024-2029)

The Ultimate Black Friday Prepper's Guide: Mastering Shopping Strategies and Savings

Cosmic Sales: The Astrological Guide to Black Friday Shopping

Legends of the Corn Mother and Other Harvest Myths

Whispers of the Harvest: The Corn Mother's Journal

The Evergreen Spellbook

The Doctor Meets the Boogeyman

The White Witch of Rose Hall's SpellBook

The Gingerbread Golem's Shadow: A Study in Sweet Darkness

The Gingerbread Golem Codex: An Academic Exploration of Sweet Myths

The Gingerbread Golem Grimoire: Sweet Magicks and Spells for the Festive Witch

The Curse of the Gingerbread Golem

10-minute Christmas Crafts for kids

Christmas Crisis Solutions: The Ultimate Last-Minute Survival Guide

Gingerbread Golem Recipes: Holiday Treats with a Magical Twist

The Infinite Key: Unlocking Mystical Secrets of the Ages

Enchanted Yule: A Wiccan and Pagan Guide to a Magical and Memorable Season

Dinosaurs of Power: Unlocking Ancient Magick

Astro-Dinos: The Cosmic Guide to Prehistoric Wisdom

Gallifrey's Yule Logs: A Festive Doctor Who Cookbook

The Dino Grimoire: Secrets of Prehistoric Magick

The Gift They Never Knew They Needed

The Gingerbread Golem's Culinary Alchemy: Enchanting Recipes for a Sweetly Dark Feast

A Time Lord Christmas: Holiday Adventures with the Doctor

Krampusproofing Your Home: Defensive Strategies for Yule

Silent Frights: A Collection of Christmas Creepypastas to Chill Your Bones

Santa Raptor's Jolly Carnage: A Dino-Claus Christmas Tale

Prehistoric Palettes: A Dino Wicca Coloring Journey

The Christmas Wishkeeper Chronicles

The Starlight Sleigh: A Holiday Journey

Elf Secrets: The True Magic of the North Pole

Candy Cane Conjurations

Cooking with Kids: Recipes Under 20 Minutes

Doctor Who: The TARDIS Confiscation

The Anxiety First Aid Kit: Quick Tools to Calm Your Mind

Frosty Whispers: A Winter's Tale

The Infinite Key: Unlocking the Secrets to Prosperity, Resilience, and Purpose

The Grasping Void: Why You'll Regret This Purchase

Astrology for Busy Bees: Star Signs Simplified

The Instant Focus Formula: Cut Through the Noise

The Secret Language of Colors: Unlocking the Emotional Codes

Sacred Fossil Chronicles: Blank Journal

The Christmas Cottage Miracle

Feeding Frenzy: Graboid-Inspired Recipes

Manifest in Minutes: The Quick Law of Attraction Guide

The Symbiote Chronicles: Doctor Who's Venomous Journey

Think Tiny, Grow Big: The Minimalist Mindset

The Energy Key: Unlocking Limitless Motivation

New Year, New Magic: Manifesting Your Best Year Yet

Unstoppable You: Mastering Confidence in Minutes

Infinite Energy: The Secret to Never Feeling Drained

Lightning Focus: Mastering the Art of Productivity in a Distracted World

Saturnalia Manifestation Magick: A Guide to Unlocking Abundance During the Solstice

Graboids and Garland: The Ultimate Tremors-Themed Christmas Guide

12 Nights of Holiday Magic

The Power of Pause: 60-Second Mindfulness Practices

The Quick Reset: How to Reclaim Your Life After Burnout

The Shadow Eater: A Tale of Despair and Survival

The Micro-Mastery Method: Transform Your Skills in Just Minutes a Day

Reclaiming Time: How to Live More by Doing Less

Chronovore: The Eternal Nexus

The Mind Reset: Unlocking Your Inner Peace in a Chaotic World
Confidence Code: Building Unshakable Self-Belief
Baby the Vampire Terrier
Baby the Vampire Terrier's Christmas Adventure
Celestial Streams: The Content Creator's Astrology Manual
The Wealth Whisperer: Unlocking Abundance with Everyday Actions
The Energy Equation: Maximize Your Output Without Burning Out
The Happiness Algorithm: Science-Backed Steps to Joyful Living
Stress-Free Success: Achieving Goals Without Anxiety
Mindful Wealth: The New Blueprint for Financial Freedom
The Festive Flavors of New Year: A Culinary Celebration
The Master's Gambit: Keys of Eternal Power
Shadowed Secrets: Groundhog Day Mysteries
Beneath the Burrow: Lessons from the Groundhog
Spring's Whispers: The Groundhog's Prediction
The Limitless Mindset: Unlock Your Untapped Potential
The Focus Funnel: How to Cut Through Chaos and Get Results
Bold Moves: Building Courage to Live on Your Terms
The Daily Shift: Simple Practices for Lasting Transformation
The Quarter-Life Reset: Thriving in Your 20s and 30s
The Art of Shadowplay: Building Your Own Personal Myth
The Eternal Loop: Finding Purpose in Repetition
Burrowing Wisdom: Life Lessons from the Groundhog
Shadow Work: A Groundhog Day Perspective
Love in Bloom: 5-Minute Romantic Gestures
The Shadowspell Codex: Secrets of Forbidden Magick
The Burnout Cure: Finding Balance in a Busy World
The Groundhog Prophecy: Unlocking Seasonal Secrets
Nog Tales: The Spirited History of Eggnog
Six More Weeks: Embracing Seasonal Transitions
The Lumivian Chronicles: Fragments of the Fifth Dimension

Money on Your Mind: A Beginner's Guide to Wealth
The Focus Fix: Breaking Through Distraction
January's Spirit Keepers: Mystical Protectors of the Cold
Creativity Unchained: Unlocking Your Wildest Ideas in 2025
Manifestation Mastery: 365 Days to Rewrite Your Reality
The Groundhog's Mirror: Reflecting on Change
The Weeping Angels' Christmas Curse
Burrowed in Time: A Groundhog Day Journey
Heartbeats: Poems to Share with Your Valentine
Dino Wicca: The Sacred Grimoire of Prehistoric Magick
Courage of the Pride: Finding Your Inner Roar
The Lion's Leap: Bold Moves for Big Results
Healthy Hustle: Achieving Without Overworking
Practical Manifesting: Turning Dreams into Reality in 2025
Jurassic Pharaohs: Unlocking the Magick of Ancient Egypt and Dino Wicca
The Happiness Equation: Small Changes for Big Joy
The Confidence Compass: Finding Your Inner Strength
Whispers in the Hollow: Tales of the Forgotten Beasts
Echoes from the Hollow: The Return of Forgotten Beasts
The Hollow Ascendant: The Rise of the Forgotten Beasts
The Relationship Reset: Building Better Connections
Mastering the Morning: How to Win the Day Before 8 AM
The Shadow's Dance: Groundhog Day Symbolism
Cupid's Kitchen: Quick Valentine's Day Recipes
Valentine's Day on a Budget: Love Without Breaking the Bank
Astrocraft: Aligning the Stars in the World of Minecraft
Forecasting Life: Groundhog Day Reflections
Bleeding Hearts: Twisted Tales of Valentine's Terror
Herbal Smoke Revolution: The Ultimate Guide to Nature's Cigarette Alternative
Winter's Wrath: The Complete Survival Blueprint for Extreme Freezes.

The Groundhog's Shadow: A Tale of Seasons
Burrowed Insights: Wisdom from the Groundhog
Sensual Strings: The Art of Erotic Bondage
Whispered Flames: Unlocking the Power of Fire Play
Forgotten Shadows: A Guide to Cryptids Lost to Time
Six Weeks of Secrets: Groundhog Day's Hidden Messages
Shadows and Cycles: Groundhog Day Reflections
The Art of Love Letters: Crafting the Perfect Message
Romantic Getaways at Home: Turning Your Space into Paradise
Purrfect Brews: A Cat Lover's Guide to Coffee and Companionship
The Groundhog's Wisdom: Timeless Lessons for Modern Life
The Shadow Oracle: Groundhog Day as a Predictor
Emerging from the Burrow: A Journey of Renewal
The Language of Love: Learning Your Partner's Love Style
Authorpreneur: The Ultimate Blueprint for Writing, Publishing, and Thriving as an Author
Weathering the Seasons: Groundhog Day Perspectives
Valentine's Day Magic: A Guide to Romantic Rituals
The Shadow Chronicles: Stories of Groundhog Day
Love and Laughter: Fun Games for Valentine's Day
AstroRealty: Unlocking the Stars for Property Success
The Groundhog's Path: A Guide to Seasonal Balance
Groundhog Day Diaries: Reflections in the Shadow
The Groundhog's Light: Illuminating the Path Ahead
Valentine's Traditions from Around the World
AI Wealth Revolution: Unlocking the Trillionaire Mindset
Love Rekindled: Reigniting Passion in Relationships
Single and Thriving: Self-Love on Valentine's Day
Emerald Legends: Mystical Tales of Ireland
Green Alchemy: Harnessing Nature's Magic
The Hearts of Horror: A Valentine's Day Nightmare

The Leprechaun's Guide to Wealth and Wisdom
Dancing with the Sidhe: Celebrating the Otherworld
Shamrocks and Shadows: Mysteries of the Green Isle
Emerald Energy: Harnessing Luck and Growth
The Gingerbread Golem's Valentine: A Sweetheart's Guide to Love and Enchantment
The Celtic Knot: Weaving Life and Destiny
Green Fire: Elemental Magic for St. Patrick's Day
Clover Chronicles: Finding Your Inner Luck
Ireland's Mystical Creatures: A Field Guide
Gingerbread Golem's Love Almanac
Prowl and Thrive: The Lion's Guide to Success
Love Alchemy: Transforming Your Life Through Heart Energy
WORLD DOMINATION: Woman's Rule 3:The New Life
The Midnight Rose: A Guide to Lunar Love Spells
The Forbidden Letters: Writing Your Own Love Prophecy
Luck and Lore: St. Patrick's Day for Modern Mystics
The Green Path: A Pagan Celebration of Renewal
The Dark Architect's Guide to Reprogramming Reality
Prankster's Paradise: A Guide to Harmless Hijinks
Manifest Your Reality: The Law of Attraction Simplified
The TARDIS Owner's Manual: Understanding the Doctor's Ship: *A complete guide to the TARDIS, its technology, secrets, and mysteries*
Starlit Romance: Astrology Secrets for Finding True Love
The Time Lord's Atlas: A Complete Guide to the Whoniverse: ***A breakdown of the locations, planets, and dimensions explored in Doctor Who***
Sweetheart Shadows: The Dark Side of Love and Attraction
February Fire: Reigniting Passion in Every Area of Life
The Self-Love Toolkit: 5 Ways to Embrace Who You Are
February Sparks: Ignite Your Dreams in 28 Days

March to Success: A 31-Day Action Blueprint
Ancient Paths: The 13 Sacred Principles of Dino Wicca
Echoes of Tomorrow: Navigating the AI Revolution
The Wellness Blueprint: Balancing Mind, Body, and Soul
Green Horizons: Sustainable Living for a Better Tomorrow
The AI Wealth Code: How to Make Millions with Automation
AI-Powered Creativity: Writing, Art, and Music for Profit
Extinction Rites: Rebirthing Your Soul Through Prehistoric Magick
Sacred Serpents tarot
Celestial Enchantment blank journal
Star Strains
Culinary Journeys: Exploring Global Flavors at Home
The Hollowvale Curse
The Hollowvale Harvest
The Egg of Transformation: Awakening Your Inner Power
Blooming Into Power: A Wiccan Guide to Spring Awakening
The Nightmare Nexus: The Third Doctor's Perilous Haunting
Digital Detox: Reclaiming Your Life in a Connected World
Ostara's Path: Walking the Spiral of Renewal
The Sacred Hare
Financial Freedom: Building Wealth in the Modern Age
Spring's Cauldron: Stirring the Waters of Change
The Hollowvale Pact
Quantum Consciousness: The Science of Reality Shifting
The Hollowvale Hunger
The Sacred Waters Within: A Witch's Guide to Hydrocephalus Magick
The Raven's Nest: Building a Life of Unshakable Stability
AI and the Human Mind: The Future of Intelligence
The Hollowvale Reckoning
Timeless Love: Building and Maintaining Lasting Relationships

The Raven's Roar: Unlocking Unstoppable Confidence
Raven Sight: Awakening Intuition and Inner Wisdom
The Butterfly Effect: Small Changes, Big Transformations
Taming the Boogeyman: How to Conquer Your Inner Fears
The Magick of Green: Awakening Earth's Energy in You
The Entrepreneurial Mindset: Secrets to Business Success
The Hollowvale End
The Shadow Luck Ritual: Reclaiming Power from Your Dark Side
Spring Magick for Beginners: A Simple Guide to Seasonal Energy Work
Doctor Who: The Hollowvale Conundrum
The March of Miracles: Unlocking Synchronicities in Spring
Unveiling the Cosmos: A Guide to Stargazing and Space Exploration
The Ultimate Guide to Surviving an Economic Collapse
The AI Gold Rush: How to Profit from the AI Revolution
Bastet's Shadow: The Hidden Power of Feline Magick
The Bastet Codex: Unlocking the Goddess's Magickal Secrets
Purring Spells: Harnessing Bastet's Healing Frequencies
Bastet's Nine Lives: Rebirth, Transformation, and Immortality Spells
Primal Currents: Hydrocephalus Magick in the Path of Dino Wicca
The Digital Gold Rush: Mastering E-Commerce and Online Sales
Future Shock: Adapting to the Next Decade of Change
The Quantum Mindset: Think Like a Billionaire
Sacred Motherhood: Awakening the Divine Feminine Within
The Mother's Spellbook: Enchantments for Love, Protection, and Prosperity
The Witch's Guide to Parenting: Raising Empowered and Intuitive Children

The Magick of Motherhood: Reclaiming Your Power Through Rituals
The Pagan Path to Self-Love: A Goddess's Guide to Worth and Confidence
Wild Woman Magick: Unleashing Your Primal Power
The Money Magnet Blueprint: Unlocking Unlimited Wealth
Biohacking 101: Unlock Your Body's Full Potential
The Wild Father: A Pagan Guide to Strength and Wisdom
The Sacred Masculine: Unlocking Your Inner Power
The Druid's Compass
The Warrior's Mindset
The Father's Fire
Odin's Path
Ancestral Bonds
The House That Whispers
The Magician's Code
The Wild Hunt
The Green Man's Path
The Altar of Success
The Shadow and the Sword
The High Priestess's Guide to Energy Healing
The Lunar Mother
The Sacred Self-Care Grimoire
The Womb Wisdom Codex
The Wheel of the Mother
The Witch's Guide to Manifestation
The Q2 Reset
The Ultimate Guide to AI-Powered Passive Income
Escape the 9-5
AI Feline Fortunes
The Tear-Stained Grimoire
Razorblade Runes
Cemetery Sirens

The Midnight Wristwatch
The Town That Forgets
AI Horror & Creepypasta
The Hollow Frequency
The Breach Echo
The Quiet Between Worlds
The Sigil of Tharan-Khul
Summon the Vault of Y'ha'ten
The Becoming Codex
The Profit of Az'ra-nar
The Drowned Logos
Echoes of the Eldritch Will
The Deep Ledger
Necronomicon of Networth
Covenant of the Wealthwyrm
The Whisperer's Manifesto
The Rites of Azh-K'luth
The Ark of the Crawling Coin
The Tithe of Shadows
Inkheart Abyss
The Timewinds of Y'ha-nthlei
The Spiral Labyrinth of Azag-Nirrh
The Gallifreyan Heresy of the Black Pharaoh
The Psalms of Nyog-Sotha
Black Rain Alchemy
The Infinite Maw
The Entropic Blueprint
The Oracle of Sh'guul
The Book of Breach
The Drowned Saint's Testament
Dreamcraft of the Sleeper God
The Silence Market
Cthonomics: The Dark Wealth Algorithm

Invocation of the Ten-Eyed King
Wealthbound to the Wyrm Below
Become the Unnameable
Codex of the Sovereign Flame
Rituals of Relentless Becoming
The Shadow Ascends
The Eyes Beneath You
The Will That Wakes Worlds
Silence Is a Weapon
The Mirror That Screams
The Whisper Between Moments
The Mind That Devours Fear
The Myth of the Finished Self
The Architect of Your Madness
The Voice You've Buried
The Discipline of Madness
Stormborn: Awakening Your Inner Tempest
The Mind That Ate Time
Unbind Your Becoming
The Pact You Owe Yourself
The Devourer's Diet
The Acid That Carves the Path
The Tower You Must Burn
The Breath Between Worlds
Speak Like the Deep
The Labyrinth Within
The Spine of the Sea God
Rejection Is a Portal
The Crown You Refused
The Scar Is the Spell
The Lightless Flame
The Habit of Becoming Horrific
ChickenJockey Chaos

The Gatekeeper Within
You Are Not Your Name
The Compass of the Mad
The Archive of Unsent Letters
What the Mirror Can't Show You
The Knife You Needed
Worship Nothing, Become Everything
The Other Voice
The Body the World Forgot
The Vein of the Void
The Black Bone Codex
The Puzzle of the Hidden Self (Millennium Puzzle)
The Eye That Sees the Lie *(Millennium Eye)*
The Ring of Return (Millennium Ring)
The Rod of Relentless Will ***(Millennium Rod)***
The Tally of the Soul (Millennium Tauk/Necklace)
The Key to the Locked Timeline (Millennium Key)
The Scale of Sacred Decisions (Millennium Scales)
Inferno Bites: The UnOfficial Minecraft Lava Cookbook
Rot in the Attic
Prana: The Hidden Force of Your Infinite Self
The Shadow Realm Within: Transforming Darkness Into Destiny
The Borderland Collapse
Claws of Protection: Bastet's Defensive Magick
Mr. Ring-a-Ding's Madness
Yugioh Astrology: Celestial Deckcraft and Duel Destiny (2026–2027 Edition)
The Seal You Signed: Unlocking the Power You Once Feared
The Puzzle of Infinite Minds: Unlocking the Mentalism Hidden Within
The Eye That Mirrors the All: Secrets of Inner Reflection
Doctor Who: The Toymaker's Broadcast

The Rod of Eternal Flow: Commanding the Currents of Vibration
Golden Eyes of Bastet: Enhancing Psychic Vision
The Key of Dual Forces: Balance Within the Polarity
The Scales of Living Rhythm: Timing the Dance of Life
The Necklace of Hidden Cause: Weaving the Webs of Fate
The Ring of Secret Masters: Rising Through the All Within All
Daggers of the Dying Deep
Bastet's Wealth and Fortune Magick: Prosperity Rituals of the Goddess
The Tide that Speaks
The Scrolls of Petosiris: 13 Rituals from the Feathered Eye
Petosiris and the Living Plague of Osirion
Feline Fire: Bastet's Passion and Love Magick
The Star Altar of Petosiris
Bastet's Whiskers: Supernatural Sensory Magick
The Bastet Grimoire
Feeding the Shadows
The Mouthless Prayer
The Spiral Wound
Becoming the Ibis: Lessons from Petosiris's Mind
The Crimson Coven: Cola Magick for Sweet Dominion
Sacred Cat's Paw
The Soda Zodiac: A Flavor for Every Sign
Covenant of the Crawling Flame
The Ink of Ish'Zur
Frothroot: The Thirst That Ate the World
The Golden Glyphs of Prosperity
The Etherbind Codex
Echoes of the Resistance: Reclaiming the You That Survived
Harnessed Minds: Breaking Free from Mental Control
The Eyes in the Smoke

Rootwake: The Carbon Covenant
Skitter Logic: Unlearning the Fear That Built You
Doctor Who: The World That Froths
Rootwake: The Fizz That Rewrites Flesh
Rootwake: Frothfather of the World
The Holly Pact: Blood Beneath the Mistletoe
The 2nd Mass Principle: Building Unbreakable Tribes
Web of Wits: A Survival Guide to Encounters with Anasi the Spider (Aunt Nancy)
The Hexbreaking Handbook: Effective Spells to Remove Curses
Pop Alchemy: Transform Your Life One Sip at a Time
The Mason Code: Leading in Unleadable Times
Petosiris and the Fifth Chamber of Thoth
The Ether Seed Within
The Parent of Tomorrow
Petosiris's Pyramid of Perpetual Wealth
Unlearn the World
Grimoire of the Hollow Tongue
Zodiac Weeds: Finding Your Strain Through the Stars
Aquarius Rises in the Bank
The Sugar God's Smile
The Skinclock Reversal: Biohacking the Face of Time
Debtburn: How to Obliterate What You Owe Forever
The Ice Cream Oracle: What Your Cone Says About Your Future
Silence Is Sovereignty: The Power of Being Unreadable
The Wind That Whispers Through Stone
Path of the Four Directions
Doctor Who: The Maestro's Symphony of Endings
Oxygen Grail: Breathing to Undo the Clock
Zodiacal Collapse: When Stars Devour Time
Teachings from the Red Sand Silence

Doctor Who: Omega – The Broken Equation

Memory Wipe Your Past: Start Over Like a MiB

Mitochondria Prime: Ignite the Core of Youth

A Nest of Roaches

Grub from the Galaxy: MiB Recipes You'll Never Forget

Whiskers of Power: Bastet's Guide to Inner Sovereignty

The Gift Must Cost Them: Negotiation Through Unequal Exchange

The Worm Guys' Wealth Code: Hustle Like an Alien

Bug Out: The Edgar Method for Ruthless Goal Setting

Weaving Life with Spiderwoman's Pattern

Doctor Who: The Rani's Renaissance

How to Get a Job (If You're a Puppygirl)

Speak Through Others: The Art of Proxy Power

T-Rex Your Trauma: Reclaim the Power of Your Primal Self

The Black Briefcase: How MiB Stay Wealthy in Silence

The Thirst Beyond Reason: Understanding Diabetes Insipidus From the Inside Out

Backwoods Witchcraft for Billionaires: The Pagan Path from Dirt Roads to Gold Roads

The Moonshine Grimoire: Fermented Spells for Abundance

The Nameless Geometry

The Wraith's Mixtape: Spellcasting with Songs of Sorrow

The Gallifreyan Gentleman: Silent Wealth, Sonic Confidence, and the Doctor's Code of Living

Sugar Water Confidence

Dino Totems: Spirit Guides from Earth's First Gods

Pumpkin Sigils & Ritual Smoke

The Hózhó Compass

The Distortus Discipline – Order from Inner Mutation

Witchcraft for the Cold-Blooded Soul

Moonlight Over the Blessingway

Water, Interrupted: When the Body Forgets How to Hold On

Deformed but Divine: Embracing Your Asymmetry

Hexes in the Henhouse: The Farm Witch's Guide to Power

The Reversed Flame: A Grimoire of Inverted Power

Salt, Cells, and Sanity: Reclaiming Balance with Diabetes Insipidus

King of the Broken: Crowning the Flawed Self

Moonlight Scars: Emo Moon Magick and the Art of Lunar Sorrow

Noose Spells: Magick of the Hanging Rope

The Goth Cathedral: Rituals of the Broken and Beautiful

The Cretaceous Codex: Dino Spirits and Fossil Magick

The Turkey Bones Ritual

Nine Lives of Manifestation: Unlocking Bastet's Reality Codes

Chaos Muscles: Building Strength from Twisted Pain

Emo Blood Magick: The Veins of Power

The 3AM Flood: Nighttime Urination, Sleep Loss, and the DI Spiral

The Silence Between the Stars

The Lemon Method: Sour Your Way to Success

Starlit Sovereign

The Rite of Twelve Gates: Walking the Gates of the Duat.

Cornbread and Conjure: Recipes for Riches and Rootwork

The Black Rose Rituals: Emo Love Spells and Obsession Magick

The Eternal Goodbye: Death Magick and Rebirth Rituals

Sinkrot: The Drain That Remembers

The Hybrid Mindset: Thinking Beyond Evolution

Bone Dry: Navigating Dehydration Before It Breaks You

Wreathcraft: Winter Sigils and Yuletide Spells

The Rite of Twelve Mouths

S'mores of the Damned: Haunted Recipes for Halloween Night

Rethink the Drink: A Beverage Survival Guide for DI Warriors

The Shadow Chord: Guitar Magick and Sonic

Malformed Yet Majestic: Leading When You Feel Wrong Inside

The Cursed Diary: Ink-Stained Spells of the Emo Soul

Anxiety Off Switch: Emergency Reset for a Fried Nervous System

The Energy Heist: How to Take Back Your Life from Drainers

Beyond the Bathroom: Rebuilding Your Social Life With DI

Coyote's Gift for Decision Makers

Ghoul-Goo: Spooky S'mores You'll Die For

Echoes in the Mirror: Scrying and Self-Destruction Magick

Thread and Thorn: Stitching Spells from Rural Cloth

The Mogwai Mind: Building Untouchable Wealth from Small Ideas

Be Your Own Guide: Trust Your Inner Compass

Hormones in Chaos: The Endocrine Puzzle of Diabetes Insipidus

ChronoCleanse: Detox Your Biological Timeline

The Limb You Hide Is the One That Saves You

Leaves, Bones, and Whisper Spells

The Dinosaur Mindset: Prehistoric Tactics for Modern Wealth

Clawing Back Control: A Bastet Method for Boundaries and Empowerment

Samhain Codes of the Forgotten

Orange Alchemy: The Autumnal Spellbook

Monster Within, Master Without

The Sigil That Sleeps

Hearthcraft: Yule Hearth Sigils and Winter Warmth Spells

Temple of the Purring Moon: Rituals from Bastet's Lineage

When the Earth Remembers Your Footsteps

Food for Mood: Eat to Heal Depression, Not Just Survive It
Witch of the Kudzu Vine: Southern Pagan Wealth Secrets
The Invisible Diagnosis: Advocating for Yourself With DI
The Coffin's Lullaby: Sleep Magick and Nightmares as Portals
Ashes of the Will: Rituals for Erasing the Self
The Fracture Rite: Shattering the Magickal Core
Funeral Candles: The Art of Emo Flame Magick
The Black Grimoire: A Blank Ritual for Writing in Absence
Phantom Thirst: A Halloween Survival Guide for Diabetes Insipidus
The Hollow Crown: Emo Royalty and Magick of the Outcast King
Sandpainting for the Soul
Falling Into Balance: Using the Extra Hour to Recalibrate Life
100 Southern Superstitions That Still Work
The DI Child: A Parent's Guide to Raising Hydrated, Happy Kids
The Jungle of Shame: Escaping the Hidden Lab of Doubt
The Witch's Toast: S'mores Spells and Creepy Confections
The Hoodoo Pantry: Spells from the Mason Jar
The Immortal Fortune: Secret Wealth Lessons from Captain Jack Harkness
The Specter's Embrace: Magick for Channeling Ghostly Lovers
Grateful Waters: A Thanksgiving Survival Guide for Diabetes Insipidus
The Seizure Gospel
Harvestbind: Autumn Sigils and Samhain Spells
Doctor Who: The Algorithmic Awakening
Silent Nights, Steady Waters: A Christmas Survival Guide for Diabetes Insipidus
The Extra Hour Effect: How One Hour Can Transform Everything

Blade Between the Breaths
Running with the Mountain Shadows
Echoes of the Failed Experiment – Becoming a Living Legacy
Swamp Witches & River Ghosts: Real Southern Hauntings
Cornbread Prophecies: Magical Recipes from a Southern Table
Doctor Who: The Signal in the Star
Bloomcraft: Spring Sigils and Equinox Enchantments
Vanisher: How to Disappear from the Internet Without Losing Your Life
The Ultimate Christmas Cookie Cookbook
The Unbreakable Parent: How to Mentally Survive Raising Kids in a Broken World
Time Debt: How to Reclaim the Hours You Didn't Know You Lost
One Month, One Million: Unconventional Cash Creation Tactics
Doctor Who: The Cyber Conversion Protocol
Black Friday Frenzy: The Art of Finding Hidden Online Deals
The Grimoire Buried Under the Apple Tree
Digital Couponing Masterclass: Your Step-by-Step Guide to Black Friday Savings
The Fire Inside the Flint
Shadows on the Ceiling: The Emo Guide to Astral Magick
The Bone-Eaters Beneath Us
Black Friday Bundle Blueprint: Creating Irresistible Product Packages for Maximum Sales
Thirteen Nights of Unbinding
Doctor Who: Engines of Influence
Pumpkin Spice Alchemy: Recipes of Fire and Frost
When Raptor Met Rexy: Prehistoric Lessons in Wild Romance
Oblivion's Candle: Burn the Path Behind You

Campfire Curses and Chocolate: A Halloween S'mores Grimoire
The Wallet That Wasn't Mine: Breaking Free from Inherited Scarcity
The Cola Zodiac: What Your Fizz Says About Your Fate
Frostfire Fortune: Unlocking Winter's Hidden Prosperity
Signal Jamming: Detox Your Brain from Info Overload
The Dust of the Forgotten Rite
The Golden Cat Sigils: Drawing Power in Bastet's Name
Mud Magick: The Prosperity of Getting Dirty
Savory Spicefall: Beyond the Pumpkin Pie
Pumpkin Spice Apothecary Kitchen
The Pumpkin Spice Economy: Turning Trends into Billions
The Ember Veil: 13 Nights of Fire Magick
Financial Freeze: When Earning Triggers Panic
The Gingerbread Alchemist: Sweet Recipes with a Twist
Biosynth Power: Programming Yourself from Scratch
Echoes from the Talking Circle
Truffle Alchemy: Fungus of Fortune
Spores of Power: The Truffle Witch's Handbook
Doctor Who: The Tower That Speaks
The Mycelium Veil: Truffle Magick Unbound
Broke But Ashamed: Healing the Shame Wound of Debt
The Evergreen Mind: Growth Through Winter Stillness
The Black Veil Truffle Rite
The Voice Beneath Symbols
Witchlight on the Bayou: Swamp Spells for Sovereignty

Get Some Tarot cards: https://www.makeplayingcards.com/sell/apophis-occult-shop

Get some shirts: https://www.bonfire.com/store/apophis-shirt-emporium/

<u>Instagrams:</u>
@apophis_enterprises,
@apophisbookemporium,
@apophisscardshop
Twitter: @apophisenterpr1
Tiktok:@apophisenterprise
Youtube: @sg1fan23477
Hive: @sg1fan23477
CheeLee: @SG1fan23477

Podcast: Apophis Chat Zone: https://open.spotify.com/show/5zXbrCLEV2xzCp8ybrfHsk?si=fb4d4fdbdce44dec

Newsletter: https://apophiss-newsletter-27c897.beehiiv.com/

If you want to support me or see posts of other projects that I have come over to: **buymeacoffee.com/mpetchinskg**

I post there daily several times a day

Get your Dinowicca or Christmas themed digital products, especially Santa Raptor songs and other musics. Here: **https://sg1fan23477.gumroad.com**

Apophis Yuletide Digital has not only digital Christmas items, but it will have all things with Dinowicca as well as other Digital products.

www.ingramcontent.com/pod-product-compliance
Lightning Source LLC
LaVergne TN
LVHW022014200926
848481LV00007B/2388
* 9 7 9 8 3 4 9 5 9 5 4 0 0 *